THE COMPLETE BOOK OF
Fashion History

A stylish journey through history and the ultimate guide for
being fashionable in every era

Illustrations by Tomski & Polanski, Jan Vajda, Štěpán Lenk

Written by Jana Sedláčková

Brimming with creative inspiration, how-to projects, and useful information to enrich your everyday life, Quarto Knows is a favorite destination for those pursuing their interests and passions. Visit our site and dig deeper with our books into your area of interest: Quarto Creates, Quarto Cooks, Quarto Homes, Quarto Lives, Quarto Drives, Quarto Explores, Quarto Gifts, or Quarto Kids.

Inspiring | Educating | Creating | Entertaining

© 2017 Quarto Publishing Group USA Inc.

Originally published as *Fashion History* by B4U Publishing, 2014.
© Designed by B4U Publishing, 2014
member of Albatros Media Group
Author: Jana Sedláčková
Illustrations: Tomski&Polanski, Jan Vajda, Štěpán Lenk
www.b4upublishing.com
All rights reserved.
Translation rights arranged through JNJ Agency.

First Published in 2017 by Walter Foster Publishing, an imprint of The Quarto Group.
6 Orchard Road, Suite 100, Lake Forest, CA 92630, USA.
T (949) 380-7510 **F** (949) 380-7575 **www.QuartoKnows.com**

Walter Foster Publishing titles are also available at discount for retail, wholesale, promotional, and bulk purchase. For details, contact the Special Sales Manager by email at specialsales@quarto.com or by mail at The Quarto Group, Attn: Special Sales Manager, 401 Second Avenue North, Suite 310, Minneapolis, MN 55401 USA.

ISBN: 978-1-63322-183-3

Printed in China
3 5 7 9 10 8 6 4 2

Contents

Don't run away!
I need to know if I'm scary enough!

Functional Furs

Humans in prehistoric times didn't have the luxuries we have today. They lived in caves or humble shelters made from anything they could lay their hands on, such as wood, straw, and mud. They didn't have stores, and were not yet able to make cloth. So what did they wear? Fur coats. Nothing is better than fur when it comes to keeping you warm. Prehistoric humans would wrap furs around themselves like a skirt or a vest. To hold it together at the edges they used pins made of bone.

Look here!
Mammoths on sale!

NEW!
Bone needles make sewing easier than ever!

First Needle

After a few thousand years of using bone pins, someone came up with a better idea. They made a small hole in a pin and were able to thread a blade of grass, phloem of tree bark, or an animal's sinew through it to stitch clothing together.

MAKING A FUR COAT

Prehistoric humans would dry the fur by smoking it over a fire and kneading it for a long time to make it soft and stretchable.

Nice coat!

Thanks. I recently caught it.

MAMMOTH FUR

LEOPARD SKIN

DEER SKIN

TRAP

DRESS YOUR WHOLE TRIBE!

I MAMMOTH
=
25 GARMENTS

HORSETAIL FURS
Hunt your own outfit!

I + I mammoth
FREE

When hunting mammoths or other large animals, hunters disguised themselves as shy deer so as not to scare away their prey. By working together, they easily overpowered the large prey.

The skins of tigers, leopards, and bears were prized so highly that not just anyone could wear them. Only the bravest hunters and most important members of a tribe could take pride in them because these skins were thought to have special powers that brought success in the next hunt.

Venus!
AN ADORNMENT FOR EVERY HOUSEHOLD

What does the ideal prehistoric woman look like? She is anything but skinny; in fact she is a buxom, motherly type. The Venus is a figurine inspired by the most beautiful models, made from a mixture of clay, ash, water and blood.

THE FIRST LOOM

Bronze and Iron Ages

When it got warmer, people stopped moving from place to place in search of food. Since that freed up their time, they were able to do other things. They domesticated animals, taught themselves to spin thread from flax and sheep's wool, and weaved fabrics on simple looms. They discovered bronze and iron, which they cast and forged to make magnificent jewelery.

 HELPFUL HINTS:
HOW TO BECOME A WEAVER

To build a loom, find three branches. Stick two in the ground and lay the third across the top. Now to start weaving, tie strands of yarn to the branch at the top. Tie a stone or clay weight to the hanging end of each strand. Now you have your warp. Thread other yarn strands through the spaces between the warp strands; now you have the weft. Continue until the cloth is finished.

FIRST PETS

TAME YOURSELF A PET

FIRST DOMESTICATED DOG

JEWELS YOU'LL FALL IN LOVE WITH! VISIT A PREHISTORIC JEWELER

Necklace made of perforated teeth
Middle Stone Age
(100,000 BC)

Beads from snail shells
Later Stone Age
(10,000 BC)

Stone beads
Early Bronze Age
(2000 BC)

Bronze necklace
Middle Bronze Age
(1500 BC)

Wrought gold bracelet
Middle Bronze Age
(1400 BC)

Wrought gold collar
Later Bronze Age
(800 BC)

Simple bronze brooch
Earlier Iron Age
(600 BC)

Gold earrings and necklace
Earlier Iron Age
(500 BC)

Gold collar and earrings
Later Iron Age
(300 BC)

ROMANTIC GIFT FOR VALENTINE'S DAY:
Necklace made of perforated teeth

It wasn't easy to drill through a hard tooth or a shell to make beads. But a skilled caveman could manage it easily thanks to a small bow, with which he spun a stick with a sharp flint tip. The cleverest cavemen went on to drill beads out of flint, then just a few centuries later they learned to melt and shape gleaming metals.

Ancient Egypt

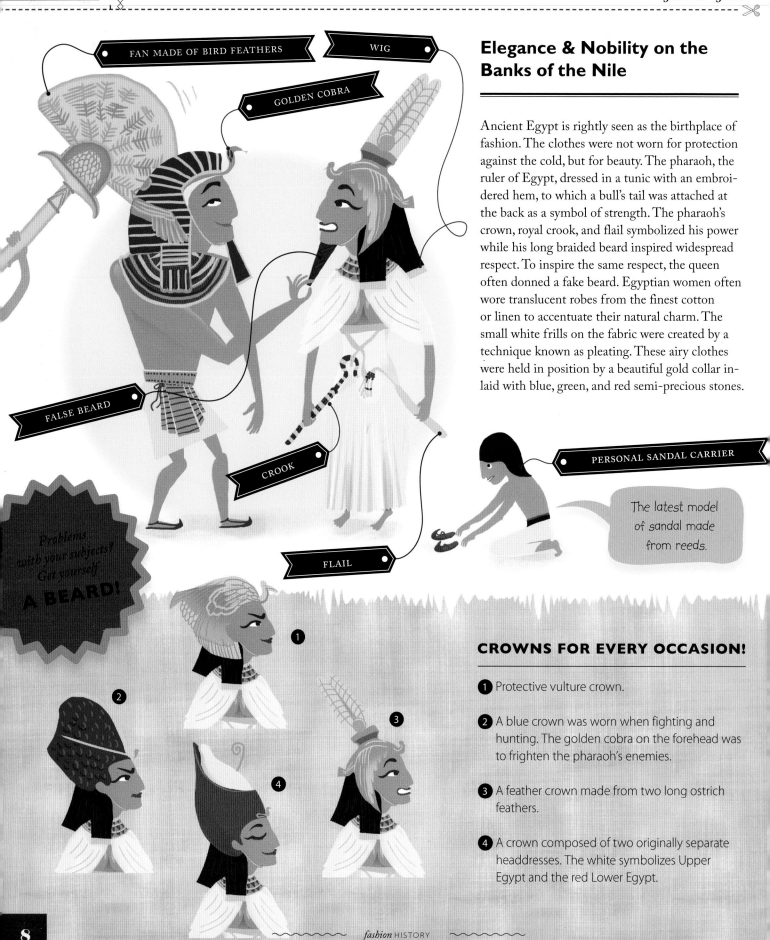

FAN MADE OF BIRD FEATHERS

WIG

GOLDEN COBRA

FALSE BEARD

CROOK

FLAIL

PERSONAL SANDAL CARRIER

The latest model of sandal made from reeds.

Problems with your subjects? Get yourself **A BEARD!**

Elegance & Nobility on the Banks of the Nile

Ancient Egypt is rightly seen as the birthplace of fashion. The clothes were not worn for protection against the cold, but for beauty. The pharaoh, the ruler of Egypt, dressed in a tunic with an embroidered hem, to which a bull's tail was attached at the back as a symbol of strength. The pharaoh's crown, royal crook, and flail symbolized his power while his long braided beard inspired widespread respect. To inspire the same respect, the queen often donned a fake beard. Egyptian women often wore translucent robes from the finest cotton or linen to accentuate their natural charm. The small white frills on the fabric were created by a technique known as pleating. These airy clothes were held in position by a beautiful gold collar inlaid with blue, green, and red semi-precious stones.

CROWNS FOR EVERY OCCASION!

1 Protective vulture crown.

2 A blue crown was worn when fighting and hunting. The golden cobra on the forehead was to frighten the pharaoh's enemies.

3 A feather crown made from two long ostrich feathers.

4 A crown composed of two originally separate headdresses. The white symbolizes Upper Egypt and the red Lower Egypt.

Eye shadow for Beauty?

Not many people know that the Ancient Egyptians wore eye shadow mainly to protect their eyelids from the hot Saharan sun, similar to today's sunglasses. The piercing eyes of the Egyptians were emphasized with black lines inspired by cats. The dark lines contained lead which researchers believe protected them from all types of eye diseases.

When a pharaoh died, all of his beautiful clothes and jewels were taken to his tomb to use in the afterlife. In order for the gods to allow him into the immortal realm, he had to undergo one last "cosmetic" procedure—mummification. First his body was dried in a salt solution, stuffed, and embalmed with fragrant oils and ointments. Then it was wrapped in thin strips of linen stiffened with resin.

Cleopatra and Nefertiti

One famous Egyptian fashion icon was Queen Cleopatra. Two Roman emperors—Caesar and Mark Antony—instantly fell in love with her. We know that she looked after her complexion using honey masks. However, Princess Nefertiti was considered to be the most beautiful woman in the whole of the ancient world. In translation her name means "the beautiful one has arrived".

No, I think I'd like some different clothes! These aren't very comfortable...

The great-grandfather of perfume

Ladies' wigs were topped with a scoop of fat with fragrant additives which would melt in the heat, releasing a pleasant fragrance into the hair and surroundings.

Magical Jewels

Many pieces of jewelery were considered magical objects or amulets. The holy scarab beetle, the Ankh cross, or the eye of the god Horus were supposed to protect the wearer and drive away evil forces. Young children would run around only wearing jewelery. Poorer girls adorned themselves with a strip of glass or ceramic beads around their waists. Meanwhile, the richer ones wore complete beaded nets over their dresses at celebrations.

BRACELET WITH SCARAB

That fragrance! It must be Chanel no. 5.

SCOOP OF FAT

ANKH CROSS

BEADED NET

PLEATED SKIRT

EYE OF THE GOD HORUS

Hey, Mom, there's Aunt Cleopatra.

When will those cakes be ready?

WIG

Trends in men's fashion

Skirt from plant fringes

Loin cloth with a piece of fabric

Come back in an hour.

Peasant

Common People

Ordinary people wore simpler clothing without decoration, which lent them a certain elegance and nobility. The majority walked barefoot, while the richer Egyptians spared their feet with sandals made from palm leaves, reeds or papyrus.

Baker

It's a beautiful day for a bath.

Cleanliness

The ancient Egyptians washed in the Nile River. Instead of soap, they used a mixture of ash and clay, and afterward they smeared a mixture of oil, honey, and milk onto their skin to prevent it from becoming dry. Although it was rare, the first underwear began to appear in the form of short triangular skirts. Egyptians shaved their whole bodies, even their heads. Beards were only grown by those who were in mourning.

RECIPE FOR
TOOTHPASTE
3.5g of salt, 7g of mint,
3.5g of dried iris
20 peppercorns
Crush and mix together.

The First Toothpaste

The ancient Egyptians suffered from bad teeth. During sandstorms a lot of sand and dust got into their bread. Not only did this make it very crunchy, but it also harmed their teeth. And so toothpaste and the toothbrush were invented. Toothpaste was mixed from eggshell, ash from ox hooves, myrrh, water, and crushed volcanic rock—not very appealing. Some ingredients went on to inspire dentists and chemists to this day!

I hope it'll help me.

Ice Cool

In this land of sand and blazing sunshine, **linen fabrics** are still popular because they are cool to the touch. They are made from the stems of blue-flowering **flax**.

RECIPE
Oil + honey + milk =
ancient Egyptian body lotion

COMB

DISH FOR OINTMENT OR OIL

TOOTHBRUSH

Musician

SCISSORS

Scribe

MAKEUP

MAKEUP PALETTE

POLISHED BRONZE MIRROR

STRAIGHT RAZOR

Ancient Greece

800 BC – AD 500

If only he sold umbrellas...

You should have worn a better himation, my dear!

HIT OF THE SEASON:
Beauty of body and soul

New perfumes from the Orient!

That Greek caught me by the beard like this and...

You have to keep up with the trends, lads!

Gosh, that oil is slippery!

The sign of a modern man: **A SMOOTH-SHAVEN FACE**

Beauty of Body & Soul

The ancient Greeks are famous not only for their love of wisdom and education, but also for their thorough hygiene. Their clothes were not complicated to make, but looked very elegant. They wore wide tunics that hitched up and belted at the waist to form attractive folds ❶. A wide-brimmed hat came in handy when travelling. A cloak called a himation looked like a light blanket wrapped around the body ❷. In bad weather, women would cover their hair with a himation drawn up over the head. Under it they either wore a light dress called a chiton ❸ or the similar-looking, though warmer, peplos. Soldiers and hunters wore the chlamys cloak fastened at the shoulder ❹.

Sports

Greek boys took part in sports from an early age. They ran, did the long jump, and competed at throwing the javelin and discus. At the Olympic Games the athletes usually competed naked, covered with olive oil so that they would gleam in the sunshine. However, they were unable to dazzle the girls as they were not allowed to participate in the games.

Warriors & Whiskers

On the advice of Alexander the Great, his soldiers shaved off their beards so that their enemies could not grab them by the beard while fighting. Starting from puberty, when they cut their hair and sacrificed it to the gods, they took pride only in a short haircut!

Spas

The Ancient Greeks enjoyed bathing several times a day. They took quick baths in the morning and then more thorough baths in the afternoon or evening.

STAY **IN** *STYLE over the coming centuries!*

4

TOP HAIR

ADVERTISEMENT

IF YOU CAN'T GO TO THE GAMES, GO TO THE HAIRDRESSER'S! Decorate naturally wavy hair with ribbons, wreaths, or headbands.

 HELPFUL HINTS: **HOW TO PUT ON A CHITON**
You'll need a large rectangular piece of material—such as a bedsheet—and two decorated clasps.

1.

Take hold of the material with both hands as though you were drying your back with a towel.

2.

With one hand bring a section of the material forward across your stomach toward your shoulder. Fasten the end with a clasp. In an emergency you can even use a clothes peg. But be careful! Do not fasten the material right at the corner, but a little further in.

3.

Now take hold of the material in the front and back where your other shoulder is. Fasten it with the second clasp.

4.

Tie a cord or thin belt around your waist and the chiton is ready.

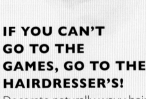

That beauty will be mine—I will captivate her with my knowledge!

Hmm, we'll see... Unlike my clothes, your thoughts aren't visible!

Greek

Roman

Typical attire

The Romans wore the toga, a splendid cloak made from an oval piece of fabric almost the length of a fully grown tree **1**! Under the toga, they wore a tunic that they wound around their bodies several times **2**. In cold weather some people would wear two! Women dressed in a square piece of fabric called a palla **3**. Underneath they wore a tunic or a light dress known as a stola **4**. A cloak could be fastened at the shoulder with a clasp, also known as a fibula **5**. Around their necks, children wore protective amulets from their parents **6**.

Dozens of Yards of Colored Fabric

The Romans took their inspiration from Greek fashion. However, they thought it was too serious and boring, so they decided to add their own special touches to it: a few extra yards of fabric, colors, and interesting borders. Roman attire was suddenly richer and grander!

Tyrian Purple

Purple was a particularly prized color. The dye was obtained from sea snails using a lengthy and complicated process and was therefore very expensive. Only emperors and senators were allowed to wear it.

LAUNDRY

The Romans were not familiar with soap. They bathed with perfumed oils and scraped off dirt with a scraper. You think that's strange? Then you probably didn't know that laundry was cleaned with either sulphur or urine.

DO YOU WANT A TIMELESS CLASSIC IN YOUR SHOE COLLECTION?

Get yourself some **GLADIATOR SANDALS!**

On their heads, Roman emperors wore wreaths made of laurel or bay leaves. In those days, the plant, which we now use to flavor soup, was a symbol of glory and victory. The laurel wreath was also supposed to protect against disaster, such as being struck by lightning.

Create ringlets by curling hair around red-hot irons.

Create the illusion of an abundant mane using a false hairpiece.

Rings

Rings were the only pieces of jewelery which both men and women wore. They were given as proof of friendship or love, and, like today, exchanged by a bride and groom. Noblemen also exchanged them during business deals and used them as seals. It was a good habit to wear only one ring at a time. However, dandies who wanted to show off their wealth might wear as many as ten! Sea corals, pearls, and amber were popular materials.

05 Barbarians

800 BC – AD 500

FUR

HOODED CLOAK

BROOCH

A brooch was made of iron, bronze, silver or gold.

STRIPS OF CLOTH

Strips of cloth were worn to keep the calves warm.

Vikings

WOOLEN SOCKS

BREECHES

POUCH WITH COMB

The practical clothing of northern tribes was suitable for all types of weather. In order to take care of their long hair and beards, they always carried a pouch with a comb in it.

Hurray for Breeches!

Greeks and Romans thought that everyone who spoke a different language was a barbarian. After making many impolite gestures and giving many mocking looks, Greeks and Romans were forced to concede that some barbarian inventions, such as breeches, were really good. Hard as they tried to resist them, comfort won out. Roman soldiers were the first to accept them; soon they were worn by other men, too. These breeches looked like two stitched-together pipes or sturdy tights. Barbarians came up with long sleeves, too, which came in handy in winter.

Barbarians vs Romans

Roman: Look, barbarians! What strange gear they're wearing!

Barbarian: Watch out, or I'll lift your skirt up!

Roman: You'd be glad of a skirt now, wouldn't you?

OK between us now?

Socks

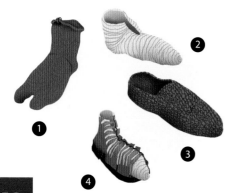

Although socks were worn by the Ancient Egyptians, it was barbarians who were responsible for a real boom in sock-wearing ❶. They spent most of their time in harsh, cold conditions, so they swore by warm socks ❷, which they wore inside knitted boots ❸. The Romans picked up the sock-wearing habit from them. Cold Romans would wear socks with sandals ❹!

Soap

Greeks and Romans had something else to thank barbarians for: soap. They no longer had to scrub and scrape themselves with sand.

Dyes

When barbarians went into battle, they painted their bodies with blue dye to intimidate their enemies. They also favored bright-colored clothing. Women would use dyes to paint their nails (unpainted nails were a social disgrace). They found their dyes in the natural world.

TORC

Celts

BRACELETS

Wandering poets, musicians, and storytellers were given bracelets as gifts.

TORC

Women and men wore a decorative plaited torc.

If a Celtic man committed a crime, his painstakingly manicured beard was shaved, and he forfeited various rights, such as the right to vote. His rights were returned to him when his beard grew back.

Land of Silk

Since there were few roads leading to the Far East, fashion evolved separately, giving rise to garments and materials very different from those in Europe, such as silk. They guarded the secret of the fine, smooth thread like the apple of their eye. Throngs of traders set out along the Silk Road for fabrics which were unrivaled in their fineness and beauty. Silk's secrets were finally discovered by two wandering monks, who smuggled the cocoons of silkworm moths to Europe in their hollow pilgrim's sticks.

PEACOCK FEATHER

The one they fit will become my wife!

The emperor awarded a peacock feather for services rendered.

EMPEROR

Silkworm

Silk cocoon

Keep up with the times! Throw away your spindle and distaff and get yourself the latest thing,

THE SPINNING WHEEL!

Spindle and distaff ✗

Spinning wheel ✓

Knots

Knotwork decorations have a long tradition in China. The thread coils into a knot, and each knot contains information. Large knots stand for important events and small knots for everyday ones.

Officials wore special hats which were supposed to prevent them from whispering to each other and influencing each other during court proceedings. If the emperor wanted to announce something important to them, he had to speak nice and loudly.

HAT

What???

OFFICIAL

Hanfu

Hanfu, the traditional Chinese garment made of silk satin, is made up of many layers. Using needles, Chinese embroiderers would decorate it with flowers, animals, mountains, and lakes that symbolize the eternal harmony of people and nature. On soldiers' clothes, there were powerful wild animals like tigers and bears, while the rank of an official could be recognized by the type of bird embroidered in a square on his chest. Gold embroidered dragons shone on the emperor's clothing, because he represented the dragon who fell from heaven, where good dragons live and bring forth beneficial rain.

Tiny Shoes

Chinese women tied up their feet into an unnatural angle to give them a miniature form. This meant they could wear tiny shoes, but it came at the price of difficult and very painful walking.

STRAW HAT

SHOES MADE OF BAMBOO

Ordinary people wore fabrics made of hemp.

220 – 589   420 – 589

618 – 907   960 – 1279

1368 – 1644   1644 – 1911

1911 – 1920   1930 – 1940

1940 – 1960   21ST CENTURY

The Immortal Kimono

Japan is a land where the past meets the present. Simple combat kimonos, samurai's kimonos and geisha's silk kimonos, have endured for thousands of years. Although these traditional garments have undergone many changes, they have survived in the wardrobes of Japanese people to this day. In ancient times, charming and clever girls were brought up from an early age to become geisha. They learned calligraphy and origami, how to play a musical instrument, flower arranging, and the correct way to serve tea at a tea ceremony. Their role was to entertain by dancing, singing, and reading poetry.

GEISHA

OBI BELT

The Geisha Look

Get a snow-white face by applying a paste made of white rice powder. Pluck your eyebrows, paint them on in red and black, and paint your eyelids the same colors. With a brush dipped in carmine red, paint on small lips to look like wild rose petals. Complete your hairstyle with a painted comb and decorated hair pins.

ADVERTISEMENT

Flip-flops Made in Japan

Did you know that flip-flops have their roots in Japan? Similar ones have been worn by geisha for hundreds of years. Under them they wear socks called tabi, which have a special gap for the strap between the toes.

DO YOU NEED TO KEEP YOUR HANDS FREE?

Get a **HAKOSEKO**! This practical purse can be conveniently tucked into the neckline of your kimono.

Do you like to clatter? Choose wooden **geta sandals**. Do you like to go unnoticed? Choose straw **waraji**!

Geta

Waraji

CHERRY BLOSSOM

SAMURAI IN CIVILIAN CLOTHES

SAMURAI IN BATTLE GEAR

KATANA

NOH

KYOGEN

Beauties from the Heian period wore their hair long and loose, and their kimonos consisted of up to an incredible 20 layers of different colors. It was very important to them to coordinate all these layers. The ideal beauty had red lips...and blackened teeth!

Wealthy diamyo lords, or landowners, wore clothes with wide sleeves. On the shoulders, sleeves, and back they often had a total of five emblems that showed which social class or family the lord belonged to. By contrast, sumo wrestlers didn't need much in the way of clothing. They put on their loincloths and off they went into the arena!

Japanese rulers were served by loyal warriors called samurai. They wore armor made of hardwood and rawhide. At their waist gleamed a samurai sword called a katana.

Let's Go to the Theatre!

If you prefer serious performances, try noh. If you like to have a laugh, go for kyogen. Whichever you choose, you are sure to be amazed by the traditional masks, which make it easy to recognize what role the actor is playing, how old he is, and what mood he is in.

This is not football, it is kemari! Players would work together to keep the ball in the air for as long as possible. In extremely long-sleeved clothing, this was no easy task!

In ancient times, men's and women's clothing was made up of two parts—a loose shirt and even looser trousers or skirt, often belted with a strip of fabric. Japanese people often wore their hair in various buns or pigtails.

Old India

BINDI

HALF-SARI

SARI

HENNA TATTOO

CASHMERE SHAWL

The Flowing Sari

India is a land of cotton, from which the majority of fabric is made today. A traditional Indian garment is the sari, a long strip of material wrapped around a petticoat, with the end draped over the shoulder or around the head like a veil. Underneath it, women wear a short blouse revealing the navel. It is still worn today on celebratory occasions such as weddings and birthdays.

Cotton boll

Since ancient times, in addition to saris, women have also worn half-saris made up of three pieces of clothing—a long skirt, a top, and a shawl, which is tucked into the edge of the skirt and then draped over the shoulder like the train of a classic sari.

BE HEALTHY - WEAR JEWELRY!

According to Indian tradition, gold purifies. This is why women wear a lot of gold bracelets and a gold ring in their nose.

Batik

Gorgeous cashmere shawls are made from the soft wool of the Cashmere goat. The material is printed, dyed, and tie-dyed. When the fabric is tie-dyed, it is first tied with string or a design is drawn on with hot wax. It is then placed in water with dye. The places which are covered by the string or the wax remain white and form a wonderful pattern.

Cashmere pattern

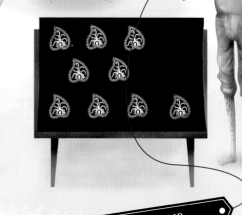

DYER

WOODEN PRINTER'S STAMP

TURBAN

ORIENTAL SLIPPERS

KURTA SHIRT

A little bit of India in every bedroom

Can you guess which ordinary piece of clothing developed from the Indian tunic and trousers? A small clue: before they were around, everyone slept in nightshirts. Yes, it's today's pajamas!

The ancient Indians did not necessarily require a needle to make their clothing. All they had to do was weave the material and then wrap it around them. The men fastened the cotton cloth in such a way that they had something halfway between a skirt and trousers: dhoti trousers developed from a simple piece of fabric wound around and passed between the legs.

HELPFUL HINTS: **THE TURBAN STEP BY STEP**

1.

2.

3.

4.

5.

6.

DHOTI

TIE-DYE BATIK

WAX BATIK

PRINTER

Cashmere goat

fashion HISTORY

23

The Middle Ages

Knights & Princesses

In the Middle Ages the slim look was fashionable. The bonnets of noble women were reminiscent of tall cathedral spires. Men wore shoes with pointed toes that were as long as short skis; so as not to trip themselves, they tied the ends to their legs at the knees with strings or chains. Knights and their ladies lived beyond the walls of stone castles. In times of peace they whiled away the hours by holding tournaments.

My lady has the glow of a church's splendid window. Wouldst I mine adversary beat, I would fall down at her feet!

HELPFUL HINTS:
CHOOSE THE RIGHT COLOR

Colors were of great importance. Ladies wore royal blue on balconies, from where the youngest of them would look out for their knights. Sky-blue expressed hope, green symbolized happiness, and white innocence.

PLUME

When competing in a tournament a knight would carry his lady's veil or chemise or sometimes even the sleeves of her dress. His plume was red as an expression of his love for her.

GREAT HELM

PLATE ARMOR

BREASTPLATE

SPURS

CHAIN MAIL SHIRT

Knight's armor was often so heavy that a rider had to be put on his horse using a special pulley. Under his chain mail shirt he wore a gambeson, several layers of strong fabric or leather sewn together in a coat. If it was also stuffed with wool flocks or flax tow, it was known as a padded jack.

GAMBESON

The Christian Church had a say in what could and could not be worn. It did not like too many buttons, tight lacing, or low necklines. In the Church's view, a lady's bare ankle was provocative.

Hi! Who wants to Know where they have the best fabrics for clothes?

Marco

NEWS FROM OVERSEAS!
Don't miss this lecture by the famous seafarer **Marco Polo!**

● LONG SLEEVES WITH TIPPETS

● COLORED TIGHTS

The high-born were keen to distinguish themselves from the poor, who had to make do with dull, dark shades of brown and grey. Few people dared walk about barefoot, as waste was poured directly from the window into the street. Stockings were mostly worn by men, ideally with each leg a different color!

All Fools' Day

Only on All Fools' Day were poor people allowed to dress like the rich and make fun of them. Otherwise a strict dress code applied; whoever did not wear the prescribed clothing could be locked up or driven out of town.

At least leave me my trousers, I beg you!

Wearing rather too many bells, aren't you, fool?!

● BELL SLEEVES

● LEG CHAINS FOR SHOES

MUST-HAVES FOR YOUR BELT

Pouches served to hold personal items, since pockets were still unknown; people also carried purses and wallets ❶. A lady would hang a small bottle of perfume ❷ on her belt, or at least a posy of fragrant flowers ❸. Men never went out without a sword or a dagger ❹.

● LONG, POINTED SHOES

THE SECRET OF A CHARMING APPEARANCE

Do not paint your face. For a fine complexion, wash in early-morning dew or rose-water. Beaten eggs are good for a tired appearance. Next time you visit the herbalist, be sure to get yourself a beeswax lip balm and camomile extract for your hair.

STARCHED LINEN BONNET

METAL CIRCLET

CRESPINE

Hair—the Crowning Glory

The ideal of beauty comprised magnificent golden locks with a high forehead and a snow-white complexion. All these things were signs of a high-born girl who did not have to work in the fields with the sun beating down on her from morning until evening. Women who wore make-up were considered proud and sinful. Maidens wore their hair loose, long, and flowing, in braids or in a bun. They adorned their hair with a floral garland, a metal circlet, a crespine, or a bonnet. Married women covered their hair with a cap and veil.

And the winners of the medieval beauty pageant are... Goldilocks for her golden hair, Snow White for her snow-white skin, and Sleeping Beauty for her rosy cheeks!

Red, blue, or green?

Were the Middle Ages Grubby?

Not in the least! Even the most stubborn opponents of hygiene sometimes splashed stream water over themselves. Those who indulged in hot baths did so in wooden tubs filled by buckets of heated water, which first had to be brought in from the well. Bathers wore either no clothes or just their undergarments. For washing, they used tallow soaps blended with roses, lavender, or almonds. They cleaned teeth with toothpicks and cold water rinses. They also flushed out remnants of food with wine. To keep their breath fresh, people chewed parsley every day.

Like women wore separate sleeves, men wore separate trouser legs. These were fastened to a belt or underwear.

ROBIN HOOD HAT

PAGEBOY HAIRCUT

HOOD

Stoat

ERMINE

Ermine

In the autumn hunts the aristocracy acquired furs, which were used to line their winter clothing. Small animals such as squirrels, martens, sables, and stoats were highly valued for their fur. The famous ermine cloak was made from the pure-white coat and black-and-white tail of the stoat.

The Fashion of Slim Waists & Round Bellies

The Renaissance waved goodbye to the simple fashions of medieval times and invited in new extravagant fashions. In addition to writers and painters, professional tailors were considered artists. A favorite material was soft velvet, which in its embroidered form is known as velvet brocade. Deep necklines were covered by translucent linens. Rich women sewed strings of pearls onto their dresses. The pointed shoes of the Middle Ages were a thing of the past, replaced by shoes with rounded tips. Queen Elizabeth I of England had a weakness for precious robes in heavy fabrics embroidered with gold and silver, lace ruffs, and the poet and dramatist William Shakespeare.

O, how well it looks with your red hair and white skin!

I love black, white, and red!

What have I been given? Stockings! Wow!

Henry

I'm terribly hungry.

I want to see more passion, Romeo!

William

PERFUME BUTTONS

LADY OF THE COURT

RUFF

ACTORS IN CIVILIAN DRESS

TRUNK HOSE

ACTORS IN COSTUME

FOR BEAUTIFUL SKIN: *cosmetics with crushed pearls!*

Essential Fashion

❶ Decorative cutouts, with an underdress peeping through; ❷ a gold-thread hairnet, ❸ a lace handkerchief, ❹ a lace-up vest.

Stockings

King Henry VIII really did receive a pair of embroidered silk stockings from the Spanish. And he prized them more highly than a coach and horses!

Leonardo

So the skirt will be a cone, the bodice a triangle, the sleeves like balls... Wait, that doesn't look right. The head is too small. Put a ruff under it!

Clothing design was governed by strict rules of geometry. The famous artist Leonardo da Vinci came to realize that the human body could be fitted into a circle as well as into a square. He painted graceful Renaissance beauties like Mona Lisa.

Pay Attention to the Line!

The ideal of Renaissance beauty was a balance between parts of the body. Corsets and bodices gave women slim waists and flat chests. A perfect line was sometimes achieved with the help of a petticoat with hoops concealed under the skirt. An elegantly dressed man was never without a round belly. Those unfortunate enough to be naturally slim wore a little light padding over the belly. Behinds, too, were padded, which made things more expensive: the owner of the trousers had to have his chairs made bigger too.

Fashion Fads

Young men liked to show off their muscular legs, while older ones wore long garments to add to their respectability. Among ladies, a high forehead was in fashion, and they shaved their heads to achieve this. A ruff—a round lace collar folded like an accordion—was worn around the neck. It looked like a cartwheel, and the head sat on it as if on an ornamental plate. The ruff was starched and supported by a wire frame so that it kept its shape.

At least I've got a cold.

Festive Clothes

Can you guess how often such clothes were washed? Never! Only underwear ever got a rinsing.

Baroque

The Beauty of Rounded Forms

Bombastic baroque was based upon an admiration of grandiose beauty and rounded silhouettes. The baroque ideal of beauty consisted of full, chubby figures. Clothes and hairstyles also had to be very lavish. In order not to ruin them, women even slept sitting up. Children wore the same clothes as adult women, no matter if they were boys or girls.

Why can't I have clothes like Dad's?

Just be glad they're not pink, little brother!

Noblemen and noblewomen wore heeled shoes decorated with buckles, bows, and pompoms. Buckles also appeared on hats, which were decorated with ostrich feathers. Clothes were accessorized with gloves, which, when thrown into the face of an enemy, signaled a challenge to make amends for an insult.

Darling, we had to get the furniture enlarged again because of that beautiful new dress you bought me.

COLLAR FROM HANDMADE LACE

Have you *seen* my powder compact?

No, I haven't, but could I borrow your lipstick?

Baroque princes liked nothing better than to organize costly balls where everyone could show off.

BRIGHT-RED LIPSTICK

PERFUME BOTTLE

POWDER COMPACT

POWDER PUFF FOR APPLYING POWDER

Moving around in wide skirts was quite challenging. The hems of the skirts were so far away that their owners could often not see them. When they sailed across the hall, many vases were sent flying. Even dancing was a tricky business—the men often complained that they couldn't get close to the women because of their massive skirts.

HELPFUL HINTS:
BE A STAR NIGHT AND DAY!

How to achieve that glamorous, attention-grabbing look

1. Apply white powder made from poisonous lead to your skin. If after repeated application your skin starts to go yellow, just apply a thicker layer of powder.

2. Highlight your eyebrows using a dark color or, alternatively, stick on strips of mouse skin. Use the best quality glue so that they don't fall off unexpectedly.

3. Twist the hair into decorative locks or wear a wig with curly ringlets. Have it made from horse hair or condescendingly allow the poor to make a little money by cutting off their hair for your wig.

RIBBON LACING

LACE CRAVAT

THREE-CORNERED HAT

CORSET

EMBROIDERED DRESS FRONT

CRINOLINE

STOCKINGS

How to Dress Properly for a Ball

Baroque clothes overflowed with lace, ribbons, frills, fake flowers, and pearls. The top layer was put on like a coat. The bosom was concealed using an embroidered dress front attached to the corset by pins. The neckline of the gentleman's coat was filled with an opulent cravat of handmade lace. Ladies' waists were brought in with a corset or bustier, reinforced with whale bone. In order to give the dress its enormous shape, concealed underneath it was a series of petticoats and a construction of hoops called a crinoline. Sometimes it was as large as a table, and the lady would have to go through doorways sideways.

UNIQUE OFFER

With these high heels, no one will look down on you! Find the perfect shoes made of velvet, brocade, satin, or soft leather with ribbons, precious stones, and pearls.

The Little Slipper Shoe Shop, 15 Golden Lane

WIDE SELECTION OF DRESS SHOES: *Get ready for the ball season!*

Decipher the **SECRET LANGUAGE** *of the fan!*

I want to talk to you.

Kiss me.

Someone is watching us.

Go away!

Don't forget me!

I love someone else.

SUSPENDER

MEN'S DRAWERS

LADIES' DRAWERS

PETTICOAT

Sumptuous dresses guaranteed by **THE CRINOLINE!**

If a lady tripped or slipped, her crinoline might ride up, revealing what was underneath from all around. Because of this, ladies wore a petticoat and pretty drawers under their crinoline. Gentlemen wore drawers decorated with stitched lace, and they tied their stockings with suspenders in the form of colored ribbons.

Masses of Flowers, Gold & Ornaments

Rococo fashion was defined by all things playful, flirtatious, and floral. Favorite colors were gold and white. While less sophisticated people continued to wear Baroque clothing, the extravagant aristocracy invented the Rococo as a new style for themselves. In even bigger crinolines and even tighter bodices, ladies looked like fragile porcelain dolls. Gentlemen wore jackets in light pastel shades that were fastened by a number of buttons and had bold cuffs. They were shaped with wires beneath the fabric so that they stuck out at the back. In combination with the waistcoat, shirt, tie, and trousers, the Rococo jacket forms the basis of modern men's suits.

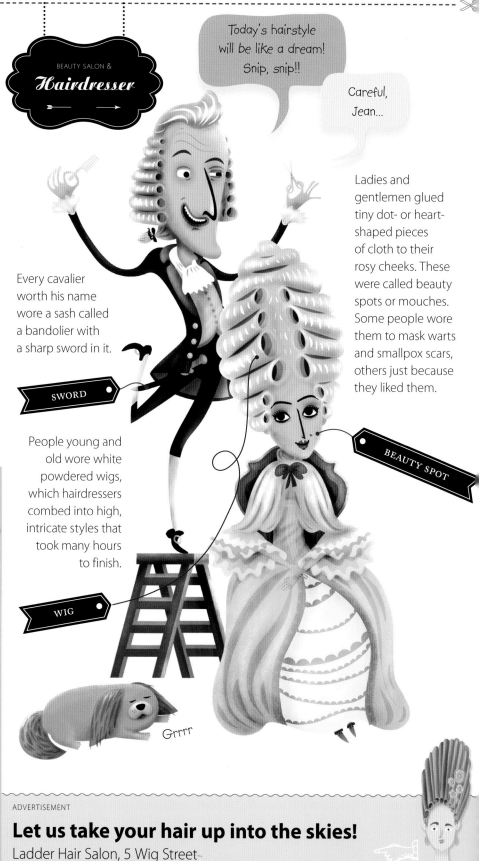

BEAUTY SALON &
Hairdresser

Today's hairstyle will be like a dream! Snip, snip!!

Careful, Jean...

Every cavalier worth his name wore a sash called a bandolier with a sharp sword in it.

SWORD

People young and old wore white powdered wigs, which hairdressers combed into high, intricate styles that took many hours to finish.

WIG

Grrrr

Ladies and gentlemen glued tiny dot- or heart-shaped pieces of cloth to their rosy cheeks. These were called beauty spots or mouches. Some people wore them to mask warts and smallpox scars, others just because they liked them.

BEAUTY SPOT

CATALOGUE
SPRING & SUMMER

Up into the waves!

Bird's paradise

Immersed in feathers

Lace fontange

Comfort first

Fruit dream

Barons & Countesses

They lived in mansions with many windows through which they enjoyed a view of a garden. At home they would wear comfortable but elegant pajamas. Their embroidered caps concealed the little hair they had left because of the wigs they wore every day. As these were a heaven for lice, ladies would carry a decorative scratcher in the shape of a little golden hand.

SCRATCHER

Bothered by troublesome insects?

Wolfgang Amadeus Mozart

Famous Figures of the Rococo

Important personalities of the Rococo include the composer Wolfgang Amadeus Mozart and Madame de Pompadour, who gave her name to a little round handbag.

POMPADOUR BAG

Splendors & Miseries of the Rococo

As doctors thought that water was harmful to health, people didn't bathe too often. They concealed the smell with a strong scent of orange blossom or apple with cinnamon and cloves. The first men's cologne was produced at the time of the Rococo, as was pomade. Makeup remover was yet to see the light of day, so makeup was just left on the face.

Empire

PUFFED SLEEVES

Hurrah, I can *breathe!*

FOLDING FAN

WAISTLINE BELOW THE BUST

LONG GLOVES

LADIES' TRAVEL CLOAK

A Fashion Revolution in Soft Colors

Empire fashion was distinguished by light, soft, and natural female beauty. Ladies cast off their corsets and could finally breathe the fresh air without restriction. People spent more time on outings, trips, and picnics. Journeys by carriage and train were also popular, leading to the creation of the first travel bags and handbags. Pale skin was in fashion. To prevent getting a sun tan, ladies wore bonnets, changing their ribbons according to the color of their dresses and shoes. Sparkling tiaras and combs or modest flowers were worn in straight hair, which was parted and curled into little ringlets.

Unlike their powdered fathers, elegant young men washed daily and spent a significant part of their day carefully arranging their cravats. They wore a tall, shiny top hat, carried a smart walking stick, and polished their shoes with expensive champagne every morning.

Young ladies liked dresses made of very light, sheer fabric, accompanied by colorful muslin or cashmere shawls. Their white wardrobe was later complemented by shades of beige, lilac, and lavender. Fine stripes and floral patterns were also in fashion. Children finally got more comfortable clothing; girls wore embroidered or lace-trimmed underpants under shorter skirts, and boys wore their first trousers.

TOP HAT

WALKING STICK

TROUSERS WITH A "FALL FRONT"

A well-sewn tailcoat with two rows of brass buttons

Get your Empire Girl! All the latest from the fashion world!

The revolution in fashion also led to the popularization of fashion magazines. Every woman wanted to know about the latest trends.

What would you like to wear when we arrive at the palace, Your Highness?

Here's a list of what's going to be fashionable tomorrow. So go on, get to it!

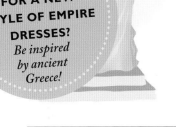

MEN'S TRAVEL OVERCOAT

The French ruler Napoleon Bonaparte was not the tallest of men. He made up for this shortcoming by wearing an admiral's hat and setting out to conquer the world. He also brought back many new fashions from his journeys. When he triumphantly returned to Paris to sit on the emperor's throne, he made the city into a fashion capital. His wife, Josephine, became a fashion icon of the time.

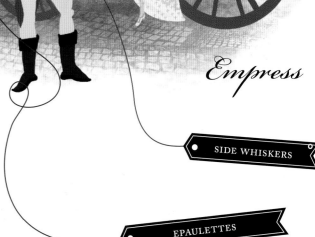

Empress

SIDE WHISKERS

EPAULETTES

Haute Couture & Wasp Waists

A true romantic spent at least an hour a day wandering, composing poems, and pondering the deeper questions of life, death, and love. In the Romantic period, novels sold like hot cakes, so it's no wonder that people's eyesight worsened from all the reading they did. Spectacles, a sign of a true intellectual, were held to the eyes by a handle. People also wore pince-nez, round lenses that are supported on the nose instead of the ears.

PINCE-NEZ

Men wore striped or checked trousers that fell over their shoes. Women longed to achieve an hourglass figure. They stuffed the sleeves of dresses with fine feathers from ducks and geese; while performing this tedious work, they whiled away the hours by telling stories, particularly horror stories.

GIVE YOUR LOVED ONE **A LOCKET** CONTAINING YOUR PORTRAIT AND A LOCK OF YOUR HAIR!

SLEEVES STUFFED WITH FEATHERS

Will you give her a ride?

I haven't got a lady's saddle.

GAITERS

DON'T MISS ANY WORLD **INNOVATION**

A pocket watch on a chain always gives the right time.

At school, girls would learn handiwork such as sewing, knitting, crocheting and embroidery. They would then use one of the first sewing machines to make a beautiful trousseau.

BOAT NECKLINE

HOOPSKIRT

BODICE TIGHTENED AT THE WAIST

BOW TIE

PROTECTIVE BORDER

TAILCOAT

Haute Couture

Charles Worth is considered to be the very first fashion designer and founder of high fashion (known as "haute couture"). This clever chap even made evening dresses for the beautiful Austrian empress Sissi. He also invented a petticoat that emphasized the behind, known as the hoopskirt. Its original steel structure was eventually replaced with padding.

Sissi introduced the fashion of the slender wasp waist. Following her lead, ladies laced themselves into corsets as never before, causing them to suffer stomach ulcers and frequent fainting fits. Some men also longed for a slim waist and would wear a corset under their coat.

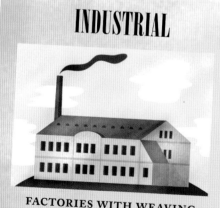

RIDING HAT

RIDING HABIT

DIVIDED SKIRT

Sissi loved to move. At the palace she had her own gymnasium, and she could ride on horseback better than many men. (She rode sidesaddle in a dress, of course.) Later, ladies dared to wear a divided skirt, or even men's trousers, to ride in the more comfortable men's saddle.

15 Victorian Era

AD 1840 – 1900

Fashionable Travel

As work was taken on by machines, people used their free time to travel and take walks in the fresh air. Visits to distant relatives were particularly popular. Ladies would take a large wardrobe with them—it was customary to wear a different dress during different parts of the day.

Please don't get dirty, darling! We haven't got a washing machine at home yet!

DRESS FOR WELCOMING VISITORS

What great steam!

PLATFORM

&

WELCOME *your husband from his travels in a new dress!*

GLOVES

PRAGUE EXPRESS

I hope that special offer still applies!

TOP HAT

SIDEBURNS

Hat Exhibition

Women and girls wore hats of all colors and shapes that were lavishly decorated with ribbons, silk flowers, and rare bird feathers. The feathers of the snowy egret acquired a value as high as that of gold! If it hadn't been for conservationists putting a stop to the hunting of their plumes, these beautiful birds would have become extinct.

Dress Codes

All skirts were long and were often worn with a short coat called a spencer. The gigot sleeves of this jacket were also known as "leg of mutton sleeves." But don't worry, these weren't slices of meat stitched together—they only looked like legs of mutton because of how they were padded.

Men, like women, changed their coats depending on the time of day. Early in the day they dressed in light shades, while in the evening they favored dark colors or all black. Men's trousers looked almost as they do today; they weren't fastened by a zip, however, but by concealed buttons. As for footwear, many men today would consider Victorian heels rather high.

Hidden buttons in every pair of trousers!

Fashion Rules

People would wear one outfit for the morning tea party, another for the afternoon walk, and a third for the evening entertainment. But the weather dictated what to wear just as much as the time of day. Would an outfit need an umbrella or parasol?

At last children were allowed to get dirty. They wore practical outdoor clothing instead of velvet jackets and heaps of white lace.

STRAW HAT

DOUBLE-BREASTED JACKET

SAILOR DRESS

PARASOL

Sailor suits were originally intended to wear on boat rides or coastal walks. People were so attracted to water that sailor suits gradually came to be used as bathing suits too.

Oh no! It's five minutes past noon and I'm still in my morning dress! How disgraceful! Children, we must hurry home!

Good Behavior

Fashion was about behavior as well as appearance. While a natty dresser at a spa would strut about in a smart jacket with a buttonhole and let others admire his looks, a gentleman would mind his manners. He may not have been so well dressed, but he always doffed his hat in greeting and wished others "good day."

Stylish velocipedists

HIGH WHEELER

BICYCLE

THE SEASON HAS **STARTED!**

A lady's cycling costume was made up of a close-fitting jacket with raised shoulders, a divided skirt, a straw hat, and high lace-up shoes.

A gentleman wore a tweed jacket with a brown pinstripe or checkered pattern.

FLORIOGRAPHY FOR GENTLEMEN
Something to say but don't know how? Say it with flowers!

Do you mean to tell me that I'm prickly and unpleasant?!

But it's a misunderstanding!

Daisy = I like you.

Red rose = I love you.

Cactus = I will love you forever.

16 Art Nouveau

Colors & Lines Inspired by Nature

Wavy lines that looked like an untamed climbing plant or a flowing lock of a woman's hair became the basis of Art Nouveau. Particularly popular were translucent materials strewn with glittering beads in unusual shades of yellow, blue, and green, as well as colors reminiscent of black tea and sunlit mornings.

Attention! **WORLD PREMIERE!**

THEATRE

BOA

Théâtre de Paris

Russian ballet **SCHEHERAZADE** **TODAY**

MUFF

HELPFUL HINTS FOR MEN
GO TO THE THEATRE
AS A TRUE GENTLEMAN!

Put yourself in a festive mood with a tailcoat ❶, a high-collared shirt, and white gloves ❷. Have creases pressed down the middle of each leg of your trousers ❸. Slick your hair down with a pomade of petroleum jelly, beeswax, or lard and add brilliantine to give your hair an impressive shine ❹. And don't forget your mustache ❺. Use special wax on this manly adornment and twirl it carefully. Crown your perfect appearance with a bowler or top hat ❻.

BOWLER HAT

TOP HAT

As fops passed through the entrance of this French theatre to see the new ballet *Scheherazade*, little did they know that their wardrobe was about to be blown away!

Flying Ballerinas

Russian ballerinas in airy costumes floated above the stage, as though carried by the wings of butterflies, dragonflies, or wood sprites. Ladies looked on in breathless amazement, some of them no doubt wishing they could cast off their tight-fitting dresses and fly free as birds like the ballerinas.

Women's dresses were composed of twenty different parts, including hidden corsets. These pulled in the hips and the waist, twisting the figure into an unnatural 'S' shape—the chest swelled at the front, and the posterior at the back, making women look a little like ducks.

Can-can

The exuberant can-can brought to the Parisian cabaret more than a revolution in dance; it introduced corsets with garters and lace knickers.

THE SECRET OF AN ETHEREAL APPEARANCE:
a hidden corset

A bold fashion, is it not?

TASSEL HANDBAG

GLASS BEADS

'S'-SHAPED FIGURE

An Icon of Design

The French designer Paul Poiret was famous in his day for his bold and imaginative creations. One of his more memorable pieces includes the feathered turban. He is considered a pioneer of Art Nouveau fashion.

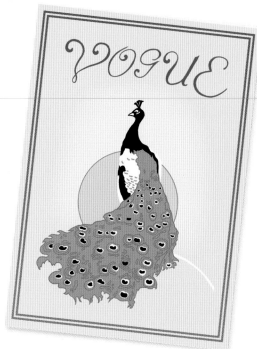

VOGUE   No / 01

EXCLUSIVE INTERVIEW!

Paul Poiret

A BREATH OF FRESH AIR FOR FASHION

VOGUE: Mr. Poiret, you have just been presented with the award for Designer of the Season. How do you feel?

PAUL POIRET: Very good, thank you. As my wife is expecting, I designed some more comfortable clothing for her.

V: Well, you did a great job: Paris is enchanted! You have freed women from tight corsets and given them clothing the like of which has never been seen before. Can you take us through it?

PP: Take my Turkish trousers and coat cut like a Japanese kimono. Both look marvellous in combination with a turban with an ostrich or peacock feather and long strings of pearls. And for ladies' feet, comfortable slippers or mules.

V: Fabulous! Thank you for the interview, and take care of your muse!

INTERVIEW   II

A Legendary Magazine

Ladies' hearts jumped for joy when *Vogue*, a magazine devoted entirely to fashion trends and fashion news, was first published in New York. It became popular quickly and remained so. Fashion lovers still read it today—more than a hundred years since the first issue.

PAUL POIRET'S CREATIONS:

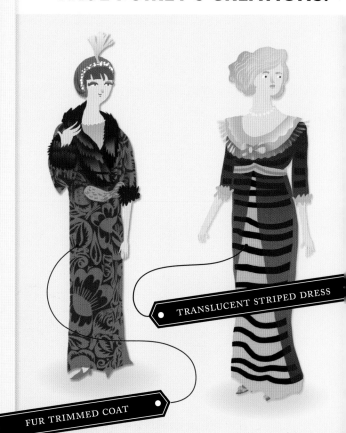

TRANSLUCENT STRIPED DRESS

FUR TRIMMED COAT

Underwear

Not all women were inclined to spend the whole day in a horribly tight corset. Fortunately, the new fashion was kinder to them, and allowed them to wear much more comfortable and looser types of underwear. Long shirts with no ties ❶ were a popular choice. Pantaloons, which were especially suitable for cyclists and gymnasts ❷. Ladies who couldn't manage entirely without tightened laces exchanged the ribcage-deforming corset for a separate brassiere and elastic girdle ❸.

Please **LOOSEN UP!**

How wonderfully comfortable!

TIP:
Show a lady your admiration with enchanting Art Nouveau jewelery!

Glittering dragonfly wings, iridescent peacock feathers, and bright-colored petals inspired not only fashion designers but also jewelers. Natural motifs appeared on necklaces, brooches, and combs.

PARTY DRESS WITH ROSES

MODEL WITH LAMP-SHAPE FIGURE

ORIENTAL DRESS WITH TURKISH TROUSERS

ORIENTAL-STYLE EVENING DRESS

FEATHERED HEADBAND

BEADED DRESS

FRINGE DRESS

Dance Fashion With a Jazz Rhythm

The First World War, a time of hardship and sorrow in which there were no thoughts of fashion, had just ended. Now people could be fashionable and dance until dawn! Heels clacked to the rhythms of jazz and the short dresses were ablaze with beads and fluttering tassels. These straight, knee-length, shoulder-strapped, waistless garments would later become known as "cocktail dresses." Women began to wear makeup again. The new fashion was bold, playful, and free-spirited.

HAVE A BALL IN A **COCKTAIL DRESS**!

It was fashionable to make dresses and hair shorter. What did mothers and grandmothers—who were still covered from head to toe in the old-fashioned way—have to say about it? More than a few girls caused quite a fuss at home.

Say cheese!

TOQUE

Every day newspapers printed photographs of robbers on the run and beautiful actresses. The latter wore their hair either in a fashionable bob or curled in regular waves.

MR. MAFIOSO LOOK

The Mr. Mafioso Look is composed of a stylish hat, white gloves, and a fashionable pinstripe jacket fitted with an inside pocket for stashing cash.

AL CAPONE SALON
entrance through the Diamond Casino
13 Confidential Street

Charlie Chaplin

Many tried to imitate the most famous comic actor of the first silent movies. There was even a "Best Charlie Chaplin" competition. The celebrated original entered this contest in secret—he finished third!

HELPFUL HINTS:
MAKE YOURSELF UP LIKE A SILENT MOVIE STAR!

Pluck out your eyebrows and draw them in again in a thin pencil line. To make your skin fairer and your eyes more bewitching, accentuate them with smoky shadows and black lines using mascara—you can get this new beauty product in selected cosmetics salons. Paint ruby-red on your lips either freehand or with the aid of a stencil.

'LITTLE BLACK DRESS'

Coco Chanel

Coco Chanel, perhaps the best-known fashion designer of all time, became famous for her "little black dress," a simple, elegant garment which today forms the foundation of a woman's wardrobe. It was worn with pearl accessories.

Jeanne Lanvin

Another well-known designer was Jeanne Lanvin. When dressing a woman, Lanvin would choose the color of a dress based on the woman's personal attributes. She didn't have much time for the new "little boy" look; her designs were softer. She had her first success with a dress she designed for her daughter—people immediately wanted it for their children too.

The Forties

Multiple outfits a day—banned. Pockets—banned. And woe unto her who is seen in a long skirt! Such a waste of material!

Elsa

Timeless Items through Economizing

In the early 1940s, the Second World War broke out and only one instruction came over the radio: save. Clothes and shoes were in short supply, and people queued for hours to get them. All clothes looked almost the same—they came in shades of dull gray or brown and angular styles, as if to imitate the tanks and military uniforms.

> **SHEATH DRESS**

> **SILK GOWN**

Glamour

Despite the shortage of clothes, there was occasionally a designer who wasn't afraid to come up with unusual designs. For example, Elsa Schiaparelli designed a hat in the shape of a shoe, which went well with a sheath dress, which certainly didn't waste fabric. Silk was used to produce parachutes, so only famous actresses could afford flowing gowns made from it. (Their timeless, feminine style came to be known as glamour.) Necessity forced women to be unusually creative. They altered old clothes to make new ones, and thought up clever ways to replace expensive or scarce goods.

A TIP FOR YOU

Do you long for beautiful eyelashes but can't get ahold of any mascara?

BLACK
SHOE POLISH

USE SHOE POLISH!

> **LEATHER HELMET**

After the War

When the war finally ended, a lot of things took on a new meaning. Automobiles and airplanes were no longer only for military purposes. Women were also as fascinated by them as men were. A number of women learned to drive a vehicle and fly a plane. When taking their place inside the cockpit, they exchanged their handsome motoring cap and wide-legged trousers for high lace-up leather boots and a flying helmet made of strong, windproof leather. Then it was up, up, and away!

DO YOU DREAM OF NYLONS?

...but you don't have the money for them? Paint your legs with makeup. Grab an eye pencil and visit your nearest beauty salon, where they will advise you on how to draw the back seams on your calves. No one will be able to tell them apart from real stockings!

Cheerful Colors

Like the atmosphere, fashion was also more cheerful after the war. Men cast off their military uniforms and went strolling in city parks wearing elegant sports jackets and low hats. Comfortable moccasins were the latest in men's footwear.

ZIP

For going on outings, children's fashion had flair. Girls wore simple dresses with collars and boys wore shorts with suspenders.

Three Cheers for Zips!

There was time for fun activities which gave rise to a new invention that made dressing easier—the zip. And it was a great success. Can you imagine what an eternity it used to take to undo the buttons on a ski suit when you needed to use the restroom?

HOUNDSTOOTH PATTERN

CARPET BAG

Is that handbag real Persian carpet or old rug?

FOX-FUR STOLE

The basis of winter fashion became coats, hats, and handbags—some even made out of old carpets.

2

PRACTICAL DESIGN
FOR FEMALE SPORTS ENTHUSIASTS!

Just untie the skirt and you'll instantly be transformed from a lady in a dress to a sportswoman in shorts!

The Fashion of Billowing Skirts

Postwar optimism swept through wardrobes with its bright colors and patterns. Thanks to modern printing machines and new artificial fibers, which were better at absorbing dyes and making them look brighter, patterned fabrics really stood out from a distance. Girls whirled around in circle skirts, dreaming that one day they would be like Marilyn Monroe. The tough-guy look was all the rage for boys: T-shirt, leather jacket, jeans and a greased-up quiff, just like the king of rock 'n' roll, Elvis Presley.

Christian

A Fashion Revolution

Christian Dior was one of the most revolutionary figures in fashion design. He was born into a family of fertilizer merchants, but he decided to follow his dream—designing beautiful dresses. He led the way in fashion with his circle skirts and thin belts, which women loved. A letter could be seen in every style. Suits with padding resembled the letter Y. Dresses with full skirts had an A-shaped silhouette, and straight dresses looked like an H.

Audrey Hepburn, the delicate, dark-haired actress with doe eyes, made this "little black dress" from the Givenchy fashion house famous. It is also the second most expensive dress from a film to have ever been auctioned. The most expensive was Marilyn Monroe's white dress.

Audrey Hepburn

ADVERTISEMENT

DRESS LIKE BARBIE!
Sensational design from Dior!

Barbie dates back to the 1950s. She was originally intended to teach girls about what was new in fashion.

Daring Coco

Probably the most famous women's suit was designed by fashion designer Coco Chanel. Women could now feel beautiful and elegant while being comfortable at the same time. Before leaving the house they could put on the legendary perfume Chanel no. 5.

Young girls went around wearing sweet little dresses with bows and dainty little shoes and socks. However, when mom was out of sight, many curious young ladies would secretly try on mom's high heels, lipstick, and nail polish.

SUIT BY COCO CHANEL

London and Milan became famous fashion capitals, a title that only Paris had previously held, thanks to knitwear. Sweaters, pullovers, and cardigans spread in popularity, as did elegant sweaters, polo-necks, and knitted waistcoats. A real obsession with knitting over the long winter nights began!

PULLOVER

DRESS WITH FULL SKIRT

ARE YOU LOOKING FOR PRACTICAL CLOTHING FOR WORKING AND SHOPPING?

A cardigan doesn't crush and is low-maintenance.

ZIP-UP CARDIGAN

TROUSERS WITH PRESSED PLEATS

Red lipstick was extremely popular. Shoulder-length hair was curled with rollers and curling tongs and then decorated with hair pins or bonnets. At work they had to tie their hair up with a ribbon or cover it with a headscarf so that it wouldn't get in the way.

After hard work, some delicious cake!

From the very beginning, brilliant whites were in fashion for tennis. Comfortable tennis shoes became increasingly popular.

During the hot summer days, everyone rushed to the swimming pool. Even there people followed fashion. Apart from the usual colorful one-piece and two-piece swimsuits, the bravest girls wore the new bikini! These initially scandalous suits were a breakthrough in the world of swimwear.

Men's trunks usually reached up to the waist, and some had a belt or a small pocket.

LET'S GO TO THE WATER!
Come and cool off and get a tan!

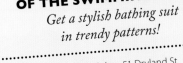

Nice bathing cap!

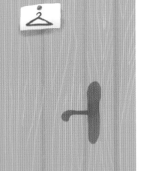

There's no one there!

A headscarf protected the head from the glare of the sun and elegant glasses protected the eyes. Bathing caps of all colors, decorated with plastic flowers or tassels, prevented even one droplet of water from wetting a carefully groomed hairstyle. The number one pattern was polka dots, with colored stripes, cherries, or strawberries competing boldly.

The Sixties

The Beatles

Anyone got a comb?

MOP-TOP HAIRSTYLE

Flower Power & Moonwalks

The Sixties were a time when ordinary people did extraordinary things. Suddenly fashion was determined by boys and girls on the street. There evolved a mishmash of styles with something for everyone. The Beatles broke the hearts of fangirls with their songs and their looks. Along with a new style of music, they introduced a new fashion trend—a black roll-neck sweater or a white collar, a chic jacket and trousers, and a well-tended hairstyle. Lovers of rougher rock made icons of the rebellious Rolling Stones, whose image centered around leather waistcoats and tousled hair.

A BEWITCHING GAZE *can be yours with false eyelashes!*

There are different kinds of beauty. Don't try to look like someone you're not!

Twiggy

The model **Twiggy** became an idol for girls. She had a boyish figure, legs like twigs, and eyes rimmed with three rows of false eyelashes glued one on top of the other.

Twiggy

The Rolling Stones

HIT OF THE SEASON:
It has to be pink!

Mothers looked at Jacqueline Kennedy, America's perfectly groomed first lady, and wished that their children—the so-called flower-power generation—were as polished.

Long-haired hippies professed love, peace, and freedom. They wore rainbow T-shirts, wooden beads and embroidered bell-bottom jeans. They loved everything natural—flowers, animals, and people.

Jacqueline Kennedy

HEADBAND

Make love, not war!

LENNON SPECS

BEADS

SYMBOL OF PEACE

BATIK SKIRT

BELL-BOTTOM JEANS

My muse! I see hats flying to us from outer space!

Pierre Cardin

Everyone looked on in suspense as humans first set foot on the Moon. Inspiration from space followed shortly after. Fashion designers including Pierre Cardin began to create clothes out of Perspex, a material made from strips of metal and plastic wrap.

SAY NO TO FURS

Beautiful actress Brigitte Bardot would never have been seen in a coat made of real fur.

She held the view that in an age of new materials it was unnecessary to kill animals for their fur and skin. She is still a passionate campaigner for animal rights today.

BE INSPIRED BY BB

Look great without furs!

Bouffant hair, playful pigtails, large plastic earrings, false eyelashes à la Twiggy—all these things were in fashion. Girls liked to wear simple miniskirts with long, colorful knee socks. Loud, attention-grabbing colors were everywhere.

BRIGHT **COLORS** FOR EVERYONE!

FALSE EYELASHES

Girls, my eyelashes are coming unstuck and I'm about to go on camera!

I'll lend you mine!

COLORFUL KNEE SOCKS

Brigitte Bardot

BB DRESSED BY THE WORLD'S BEST DESIGNERS

1 This dress made of small metal discs was designed by Paco Rabanne. **2** This transparent dress is the work of fashion designer Yves Saint-Laurent. **3** This paper dress indicates that fashion is beautiful but short-lived. **4** Op art for lovers of mathematics and geometry, by André Courrèges. **5** Pop art for avid readers of comic books.

The Seventies

DISCO!
On Platforms
in the Spotlight

If the fashions of the Sixties seem eccentric to you, take a look at what people wore ten years later! The ideal material was artificial, elastic, and shiny. Clothes either glittered with sequins, or popped with vibrant colors. Spacesuits were still in fashion. Fashion experiments in the Seventies went so far that the decade became known as the "tasteless decade" and the style was called "anti-fashion."

Show me what you wear and I'll tell you what music you listen to. People wore a wide variety of clothes, which reflected the variety of musical styles.

FUNKY

BREAK DANCE

POP

High platform shoes were practical as well as fashionable: when the wearer walked through a puddle, the foot remained dry. Jeans mania swept across the world. Previously, blue denim had been work attire for cowboys, but the seventies made it a material for jackets, dresses, skirts, trousers, and more.

DISCO

PLATFORMS

Vivienne Westwood

DESTROY

PUNK, PUNK, PUNK!

Going Against the Flow

Not everyone loved the garish fashions of disco. Some people felt the need to differentiate themselves from the majority not only with new styles of music but also by appearance. Designer Vivienne Westwood found inspiration in things that others rejected. She and other adherents of punk made ripped T-shirts, tartan skirts, fishnet stockings, and leather jackets studded with pins fashionable.

EVERYONE
LOVES
MUSIC

GOTH

INDIE

ROCK

Blazin' suit!

PUNK

COUNTRY

AFRO

BELL SLEEVES

JUMPSUIT

The bell became a popular shape—there were bell-bottom trousers and shirts and blouses with bell sleeves. Fashion hits included jumpsuits and Afro hairdos. Men showed off their bare chests in clothes with low necklines, like the singer David Bowie. He even complemented his flamboyant costumes with striking makeup.

David Bowie

Plastic Mania

Stylish ladies wore pumps, shiny tights, and broad-shouldered gray suit-jackets to work. Had her afternoon workout routine given her such big muscles? Of course not—jackets and blouses had shoulder pads! Men wore ties and suspenders with shirts tucked into trousers paired with crocodile-skin moccasins. Fortunately for crocodiles, the leather was mostly imitation.

A HOLE IN YOUR T-SHIRT?

An embarrassment? On the contrary, it's dernier cri, *or the latest in fashion!*

Jeans shrunk around the ankles— bell bottoms gave way to drainpipes. The best jeans looked as though they had spent a month going moldy in a dank cellar.

SHOULDER PADS

HOLEY T-SHIRT

CROCODILE-SKIN HANDBAG

CROCODILE-SKIN MOCCASINS

MARBLE-WASH JEANS

DENIM JACKET

Work Out Wherever You Can!

Roller skates and aerobics were hugely popular. It was a must to have an elastic headband ❶ and a matching tracksuit ❷, supplemented with a rucksack and a fanny pack ❸ in bright colors. Sneakers ❹, ideally with fluorescent laces, looked great with all this.

Elastic leggings in fluorescent colors ❺ were worn for exercise and under ruffle skirts. Leg warmers ❻ came in handy when the weather was bad. Leggings printed with multicolored patterns looked great with a wide varnished belt or a crop top.

Only a digital watch gives you the exact time. Choose one to match your nails!

When girls took a walk at sunset, it was essential that they wore Romantic-style dresses and bold lipsticks in shades ranging from pale pink to burgundy red. Boys dazzled girls by wearing a sweater draped casually over the shoulder—which allowed them to offer their date protection against the cold at any time.

Lion's mane

Those who had naturally big hair were onto a winner. Those who didn't had their hair artificially curled in a permanent wave. Men went in for this too, leaving their hair short at the top and long at the neck. The most fashionable hair color was blond.

Michael Jackson

The singer and dancer Michael Jackson, known as the king of pop, was a genius of not only rhythm, but also fashion. Today we would raise an eyebrow at black loafers worn with white socks, but in the Eighties, Jackson's style was copied by thousands of fans.

Plastic forever!

Want to be trendy? Throw away your gold and buy these indispensable items:

- heart-shaped glasses
- star earrings
- smiley badges
- plastic bangles and rings
- friendship bracelets
- charm necklaces

CURLERS

FINGERLESS GLOVES

LION'S MANE

BALLOON SKIRT

TULLE SKIRT

RUBBER SANDALS

PLASTIC HANDBAG

The Nineties

London Style!

The Nineties were marked by loose, comfortable clothing that people could wear in the city, or for a picnic. Denim trousers, dresses, and hats were still hugely popular. The Walkman, the great-grandfather of today's MP3 players, was a hit with children and youngsters; it played their favorite music on audio cassette.

HIT OF THE SEASON: *denim!*

BAD-WEATHER OUTFIT

WALKMAN

BASEBALL CAP

OVERALLS

DENIM DRESS

London youth came up with a style known as 'grunge'. The principle was simple: to look as though you didn't care. Their parents had a rather different view: they thought their kids looked like they had just crawled out of a trash can!

GRUNGE IS IN!

FLANNEL SHIRT

TORN JEANS

Marc Jacobs

Young designers had an interest in careless fashion too. Marc Jacobs designed a number of (expensive) items in this style … and was given the boot! The fashion house he worked for told him that only a fool would pay such money for rags. But then shabby grunge caught on with celebrities!

To be grunge, get yourself:

- a faded second-hand T-shirt
- a flannel shirt to tie around your waist
- frayed jeans, torn shorts, or a checkered skirt
- long, bedraggled hair with a backward baseball cap and round glasses
- Converse canvas sneakers or heavy-duty Dr. Martens shoes

DR MARTENS SHOES

CONVERSE SNEAKERS

Madonna Mia!

The flamboyant outfit of pop singer Madonna, with its cone bra and ponytail, became a symbol of the time. It was designed by Jean Paul Gaultier.

Jean Paul

Meet the queen of pop!

DENIM HAT

Those who weren't grunge could let their imaginations run wild. Here are some popular looks:

1 high pigtails,
2 a palm tree in the middle of the head,
3 topknots and fashionable John Lennon specs,
4 butterfly clips and glitter eye makeup,
5 a head full of braids and beads, bright-blue eyelashes and a choker around the neck!
6 Boys experimented with shavers, perms, gels and bleaches. Many a sheep must have envied those curls.

SCHOOL

Back to your desks, girls!

FRIZZY HAIR

To get a fashionable frizzy hairstyle, just shake out your hair!

Has time stood still?

A Unique Mixture

Today's fashion changes from one day to the next. What was popular yesterday might not be popular today. But the good thing is that no one has to make changes to their wardrobe if they don't want to. Girls aren't required to wear frilly dresses, and boys aren't expected to wear jackets and bow ties. Everyone can choose what suits them best or simply what they like. Fashion is free: you should feel comfortable in what you wear, regardless of whether you are exercising or going to a party.

Some designs are strikingly familiar, aren't they? Almost everything that is worn today has been worn at some time in the past.

The modern man's suit **1** hasn't changed much since Victorian times and the roaring Twenties. How many minutes have passed since that chap in Romanticism looked at his pocket watch?

Japanese youth fashion has moved a long way from the traditional kimono of the samurai and the geisha. Their platform shoes **2** go back to the Seventies, and can even be linked to ancient China!

Women wore corsets **3** from the Renaissance to the Art Nouveau age. Although in the past corsets were underwear, these days they adorn party dresses.

Jeans and the peaked cap that first saw the light of day in the Fifties are still popular. **4**

Unisex fashion **5** is for girls and boys.

The checkered **6** shawls of the ancient barbarians influence today's patterns.

Classics never go out of fashion. Hand-held bags **7** have been around since Empire times, as have dresses cut below the bosom **8**.

Retro fashion (also known as vintage) **9** is so popular that it keeps coming back. These polka dots were trendy in the Fifties.

The first high-heeled shoes were from the Renaissance! **10**

COLORED NAILS? THE CELTS KNEW HOW TO DO THESE!

Eco Fashion

Environmentally friendly clothing is kind to nature. It is often made of natural materials such as cotton, wool, and linen. It also includes jeans and bags produced from recycled PET bottles or chocolate bar wrappers.

ECO T-SHIRT

Zippers

Today we can't imagine clothes without easy-fastening zips. Fortunately the zipper has been around for some time—since the Forties at least!

EYE SHADOW?
That's nothing new. In fact the Ancient Egyptians used it!

12

13

HAS SOMEONE STOLEN YOUR CLOTHES? YOU DON'T KNOW WHAT TO WEAR?

Spray-on clothing meets all your fashion needs! And you can wipe it off whenever you want, and create another great design.

FASHION WITHOUT ORDERS

With Alexander McQueen's butterfly hat, your ideas won't fly off in all directions!

The cat express?

9

Hipsters **11** revive fashions of the good old days. They love all that is retro, old bicycles, and cats.

Harem pants **12** inspired by the Orient look great with stylish flip-flops— which could have come to us from ancient Japan **13**.

Don't forget what the English poet Percy Bysshe Shelley used to say:

"You're never fully dressed without a smile."

11

Fashion of the Future

Maybe one day we'll wear intelligent clothing that will fasten and unfasten depending on the weather, like the futuristic designs of Hussein Chalayan. These clothes could even be powered by the energy we generate while walking.

10

HIPSTER

Let's remember how fashion has changed over time and across continents.

PREHISTORY

ANCIENT EGYPT

ANCIENT ROME

ANCIENT GREECE

BARBARIANS

OLD CHINA

OLD JAPAN

OLD INDIA

RENAISSANCE

MIDDLE AGES

BAROQUE

ROCOCO

69

FIFTIES

SIXTIES

EIGHTIES

SEVENTIES

NINETIES

PRESENT DAY

Be inspired... by women who set the tone for contemporary fashion.

Jennifer Lopez
She likes bright colors and figure-hugging designs that accentuate the feminine.

Victoria Beckham
Her own designs radiate self-confidence and simplicity.

Rihanna
Her fashion is bold and playful. She is like a chameleon: you never know what she'll surprise you with next!

Kate Moss
She knows that black is chic! Apart from black, she has a liking for animal patterns and men's hats.

Mary-Kate & Ashley Olsen
These sisters are fans of non-traditional, Bohemian styles with added oomph from playful, fun accessories.

Lady Gaga
She likes to provoke and cross fashion boundaries. She calls herself a walking piece of art.

Anne Hathaway
She has a subtle, boyish style of dress.

Kate, Duchess of Cambridge
Her favorite elegant designs include classic jackets accessorized with fetching hats.

Michelle Obama
America's former first lady believes in elegance and comfort. She's not afraid of vivid colors.

Swimwear

300 BC   1830   1870

1930   1920   1900   1890

1935   1945   1955   PRESENT DAY

Ladies' Hats

MIDDLE AGES ---- RENAISSANCE ---- BAROQUE ---------- EMPIRE ---- VICTORIAN ERA ---- 1920

PRESENT DAY ---- 1990 ---------- 1970 ---- 1950 ---------- 1940 ---------- 1930

Hairstyles

ANCIENT EGYPT ---- MIDDLE AGES ---- RENAISSANCE ---- ROCOCO ---------- EMPIRE ---- ART NOUVEAU

1990 ---- 1980 ---------- 1970 ---------- 1960 ---------- 1940 ---------- 1920

Wedding Dresses

EMPIRE — ROMANTICISM — VICTORIAN ERA — ART NOUVEAU

1960 — 1950 — 1930 — 1920

1970 — 1980 — 1990 — PRESENT DAY

MIDDLE AGES ---- ROCOCO ---- EMPIRE ---- ROMANTICISM

1940 ---- 1920 ---- ART NOUVEAU ---- VICTORIAN ERA

1950 ---- 1960 ---- 1970 ---- 1980

TOP 10 *Handbags You Need to Know*

Louis Vuitton Speedy 30

Alexander McQueen Skull Clutch

Longchamp Tote Bag

Fendi Baguette

Bottega Veneta Campana

Chloé Paraty

Hermès Birkin

Lady Dior

Mulberry Alexa

Chanel 2.55

ANCIENT EGYPT --- ANCIENT ROME --- MIDDLE AGES --- RENAISSANCE --- BAROQUE

1930 --- 1920 --- ART NOUVEAU --- VICTORIAN ERA --- EMPIRE

1950 --- 1960 --- 1970 --- 1980 --- 1990

PRESENT DAY

Shoes You Need to Know

Vivienne Westwood   Charlotte Olympia   Christian Louboutin   Giuseppe Zanotti   Melissa by V. Westwood

Joanne Stoker   Alexander McQueen   Jimmy Choo   Antonio Berardi   Manolo Blahnik

Jean Paul Gaultier

Calvin Klein

Hussein Chalayan

Alexander McQueen

Valentino

Ralph Lauren

Versace

John Galliano

Yves Saint-Laurent

Coco Chanel

Karl Lagerfeld

Marc Jacobs

Mary Quant

Pierre Cardin

Giorgio Armani

Christian Dior

Givenchy

Issey Miyake

Vivienne Westwood

Vera Wang

Stella McCartney